Edward Bouverie Pusey, Henry Parry Liddon

The Purchas Judgment

A Letter of Acknowledgment to the Right Hon. Sir J.T. Coleridge

Edward Bouverie Pusey, Henry Parry Liddon

The Purchas Judgment
A Letter of Acknowledgment to the Right Hon. Sir J.T. Coleridge

ISBN/EAN: 9783337067656

Printed in Europe, USA, Canada, Australia, Japan

Cover: Foto ©ninafisch / pixelio.de

More available books at **www.hansebooks.com**

THE

PURCHAS JUDGMENT

A Letter of Acknowledgment

TO THE

RIGHT HON. SIR J. T. COLERIDGE

*One of the Lords of Her Majesty's Most Honourable
Privy Council*

BY H. P. LIDDON, D.D. D.C.L.

PROFESSOR OF EXEGESIS AT OXFORD, AND CANON OF ST. PAUL'S

Together with a Letter to the Writer

BY THE REV. E. B. PUSEY, D.D.

REGIUS PROFESSOR OF HEBREW AND CANON OF CHRIST CHURCH

London

RIVINGTONS, WATERLOO PLACE

HIGH STREET	TRINITY STREET
Oxford	Cambridge

1871

My dear Sir John Coleridge,

When you do me the great honour to address me in public, it is, I trust, needless for me to say that you are justified in assuming that I shall read whatever you may write with the most respectful attention, and that if I am unable to follow you in every particular, it will always be with great hesitation and regret that I shall admit this inability to myself. Apart from some kindnesses of a more personal character, and of which I cherish a grateful memory, you have one claim upon me, as upon many others, which certainly does not grow weaker with the lapse of time. You have made the character, the work, the home of the best and wisest man whom I have ever known intimately in life, the common property of his countrymen. In your Memoir of my most revered and beloved friend, there are, as I venture to think, some features of his later mind (I can speak of nothing more), which might have been somewhat differently handled by younger men, who cross-questioned him as a Teacher while they had the opportunity of doing so. But, as a contemporary and an equal, you naturally took much for granted; while you alone could give us his life, as a whole, from actual knowledge of him, and with the authority of a position which is above discussion.

Certainly, the conviction that he would not have been altogether silent at such a painful crisis as that which has been created by the recent judgment, was not among the least constraining of the motives which induced me, hesitatingly and unwillingly enough, to join in the chorus of protests with which it ·has been received. For this judgment does not merely help to fulfil that anticipation of his, to which I have already referred, namely, " that we shall never have God's blessing on our work in the Church of England while we continue quietly to acquiesce in the present constitution of the Court of Final Appeal." It illustrates his foresight even more strikingly in another respect. A friend had been saying to him, that if the Judicial Committee strained the formularies in one direction to admit of the denial of Baptismal Grace, and in another to sanction denials of the Inspiration of Scripture and of the endlessness of future punishment, it would at least be consistently tolerant towards High Churchmen, should they hereafter be prosecuted by their theological opponents. " I am not at all sure of that," he said; " the same instinct which strains the formularies in order to screen misbelief or unbelief, may narrow them so as to proscribe a strong and clear faith, or that which implies it." These were, I believe, his very words; and we have not had to wait long in order to understand their sagacity.

For that the late judgment does adopt a construction of the documents before the Court which is, to say the least, not the most obvious one, is clearly your own opinion. You " think Mr. Purchas has not had justice done to him in two main points of the late appeal."[1] Referring to the " Ornaments Rubric," you justify this opinion in the following terms:—

" Mr. Purchas has been tried before the Committee for offences alleged to have been committed against the provisions of the ' Act of Uniformity : ' of this Act the Common Prayer Book is part and parcel. As to the vestments, his conduct was alleged to be in derogation of the Rubric as to the ornaments of the Church and the Ministers thereof, which ordains that such shall be retained and be in use as were in this Church of England by the authority of Parliament in the second year of the reign of King Edward VI.

"The Act of Uniformity is to be construed by the same rules exactly as any Act passed in the last Session of Parliament. The clause in question (by which I mean the Rubric in question) is perfectly unambiguous in language, free from all difficulty as to construction ; it therefore lets in no argument as to intention other than that which the words themselves import. There might be a seeming difficulty in *fact*, because it might not be known what vestments were in use by authority of Parliament in the second year of the reign of King Edward VI. ; but this difficulty has been removed. It is conceded in the Report that the vestments, the use of which is now condemned, were in use by authority of Parliament in that year. Having that fact, you are bound to construe the Rubric as if those vestments were specifically named in it, instead of being only referred to. If an Act should be passed to-morrow that the uniform of the Guards should henceforth be such as was ordered for them by authority, and used by them in the 1st Geo. I., you would first ascertain what that uniform was ; and, having ascertained it, you would not inquire into the changes which may have been made, many or few, with or without lawful authority, between the 1st Geo. I. and the passing of the new Act ? All these, that Act, specifying the earlier date, would have made wholly immaterial. It would have seemed strange, I suppose, if a commanding officer, disobey-

---

ing the statute, had said in his defence—'There have been many
changes since the reign of Geo. I. ; and as to " retaining," we put
a gloss on that, and thought it might mean only retaining to the
Queen's use ; so we have put the uniforms safely in store.' But,
I think, it would have seemed more strange to punish and mulct
him severely if he had obeyed the law and put no gloss on plain
words.

"This case stands on the same principle. The Rubric indeed
seems to me to imply with some clearness that in the long in-
terval between Ed. VI. and the 14th Ch. II. there had been many
changes ; but it does not stay to specify them, or distinguish between what was mere evasion and what was lawful : it quietly
passes them all by, and goes back to the legalized usage of the
2nd year of Ed. VI. What had prevailed since, whether by an
Archbishop's gloss, by Commissions or even Statutes, whether,
in short, legal or illegal, it makes quite immaterial.

"I forbear to go through the long inquiry which these last
words remind one of—not, I am sure, out of any disrespectful
feeling to the learned and reverend authors of the Report, but because it seems to me wholly irrelevant to the point for decision.

"This alone I must add, that even were the inquiry relevant,
the authorities on which they rely do not appear to me so clear
or cogent, nor the analogies relied on so just, as to warrant the
conclusion arrived at. For it should never be forgotten that the
defendant in a criminal case, acquitted as to this charge by the
learned Judge below, was entitled to every presumption in his
favour, and could not properly be condemned but by a judgment
free from all reasonable doubt. And this remark acquires additional strength, because the judgment will be final, not only on
him but the whole Church for all time, unless reversed by the
Legislature." [1]

It is difficult to understand how, if the Court had
approached the question before it in the disinterested
spirit of an entirely impartial criticism, it could
have dealt so summarily with the Ornaments Rubric.
For this Rubric, besides forming part of the Ritual
law of the Church, is a clause in an Act of Parlia-

[1] Remarks, pp. 7–9.

ment. Will it not be necessary to determine what legal effect remains to this " clause " since the date of the recent decision ? And if it should appear that the judgment has practically destroyed its legal effect, what will be said of the appeal to Royal advertisements and Ecclesiastical canons by which this clause of the Act has been emptied of its force —canons and advertisements which were under the eyes of the Parliament which passed the Act in which the clause occurs ? What would have been said if a decision, based on such an appeal, had been given in a civil case, or against the popular side in the Church ? Certainly it is not for clergymen to depreciate the authority of the canons ; but that they should have been appealed to in order to neutralize the plain sense of an Act of Parliament must, it might be supposed, occasion considerable surprise to all independent lawyers.

As to the position of the celebrant in the service of the Holy Communion, you do not think that the report of the Judicial Committee " can be shown conclusively to be wrong." But neither do you think that it " can be shown conclusively to be right." I understand you to mean that the ' failure of justice ' here consists in an attempt to close a question which, if the Rubric is to rule, ought to be left open. You observe :—

" In my opinion, on such a question as this, where a conclusion is to be arrived at upon the true meaning of Rubrics framed more than two centuries since, and certainly not with a view to any such minute criticism as on these occasions is and must bo applied to them, and where the evidence of facts is by no means clear, none probably can be arrived at free from reasonable objection. What is the consequence? It will be asked, Is the question to receive no judicial solution? I am not afraid to answer. Better far that it should receive none than that injustice should be done. The principles of English law furnish the practical solution: dismiss the party charged, unless his conviction can be based on grounds on which reasonable and competent minds can rest satisfied, and without scruple. And what mighty mischief will result to countervail the application of this rule of justice? For two centuries our Church has subsisted without an answer to the question which alone gives importance to this inquiry; and surely has not been without God's blessing for that time, in spite of all much more serious shortcomings." [1]

At the risk of going over what has now become sufficiently familiar ground, I will here quote the language of a member of the Lower House of Convocation, whose intimate acquaintance with questions of this description is generally acknowledged :—

" On the 23rd of December, 1868," he says, " the Judicial Committee, in delivering judgment (Martin *v.* Mackonochie), quoted the following Rubric before the Prayer of Consecration in the Communion office,—' When the Priest, standing before the table, hath so ordered the bread and wine that he may with the more readiness and decency break the bread before the people and take the cup into his hands, he shall say the Prayer of Consecration as follows '—and then the Court proceeded thus to interpret this instrument: ' Their lordships entertain no doubt on the construction of this Rubric, that the priest is intended to continue in one posture during the prayer, and is not to change from standing to kneeling or *vice versa*. And it appears to them equally certain that the priest is intended to stand and not to kneel. *They think that the words " standing before the table " apply to the whole sentence.*' Having made some further remarks their lordships then added what had been already before laid down by the Court, to which they were disposed entirely to adhere, viz., that 'in the performance of the services, rites, and ceremonies, ordered by the Prayer Book, the directions contained in it must be strictly observed; no omission and no addition can be permitted.'

---

[1] Remarks, p. 9.

" But though the Judicial Committee on December 23rd, 1868, affirmed that in the judgment of the Court, then indeed entertained without a doubt, the words ' standing before the table ' applied to ' the whole sentence' which contains the directions for saying the Prayer of Consecration, yet that same tribunal, on February 23rd, 1871, decided that the Prayer of Consecration is to be used at the ' north side of the table' *i. e.*, in a totally different position— thus not only contradicting its own previous judgment, entertained at the time of its delivery without any doubt, but also ignoring the distinction maintained in the Latin Rubric and expressed by the words '*ante mensam*' and '*coram populo.*' And once again, though the Judicial Committee twice over, viz., on March 21st, 1857, and on December 23rd, 1868, decided that the 'directions contained' in the Prayer Book 'must be strictly observed, no omission, no addition ' ' can be permitted ' — yet that same tribunal on February 23rd, 1871, gave a judgment announcing its determination to advise her Majesty that a monition should issue against a clergyman, bidding him to desist from observing ' the directions contained ' in the Prayer Book which, according to the previous ruling of their lordships, ' he had strictly observed ' by saying the Prayer of Consecration ' standing before the table,'—and after having ordered the Elements by abstaining from a change of position (for a ceremonial reason now suggested by the Court) from the west to the north side of the table. Such change, moreover, being manifestly 'an addition' to the directions of the Prayer Book which the Court in two previous judgments had decided, could not ' be permitted.' " [1]

In short, whatever may be the true law of the case, the Judicial Committee would here appear to have given two decisions which rest upon contradictory constructions of a single sentence. The words " standing before the table " do govern the whole Rubric in which they occur, or they do not govern it. If they do not, Mr. Mackonochie was not wrong in kneeling at any time during the Prayer of Consecration. But, it having been decided that the words

[1] Rev. James Wayland Joyce, letter of March 6, 1871, inserted in the *John Bull* and *Church Times.*

in question do govern the Rubric throughout, and
that therefore Mr. Mackonochie had no legal right
to kneel at any time during the Prayer of Consecration, Mr. Purchas surely obeyed the law in " standing
before the table " during the Prayer of Consecration.
It is pleaded that, in the case of Mr. Mackonochie,
the kneeling or standing posture of the celebrant
was alone before the Court ; while, in Mr. Purchas's
case, the celebrant's position relatively to the Holy
Table was alone before them.   But this plea does
not justify two contradictory constructions of the
same words.   The true construction cannot depend
upon " the question before the Court," since it is
itself strictly a question of grammatical truth ; and if
rightly decided once, is decided once for all.   It is
not argued that the word " standing " applies to the
whole Rubric, while the words " before the table "
do not.   The escape from the difficulty is held to lie
in the sense of the preposition "before."   Their
Lordships say that " the words ' before the table ' do
not necessarily mean between the table and the
people, and are not intended to limit to any side."[1]
Practically, " they think that the Prayer of Consecration is to be used at the north side of the table,
so that the minister looks south."[2]   " Before the
table," then, means, in the judgment of their Lordships, " at the north end of" the table ; and this
sense is imposed upon the preposition " before " by

[1] Judgment of the Judicial Committee of the Privy Council in
the case of Hebbert *versus* Purchas.   Edited by Edward Bullock,
Esq., p. 38.
[2] Ibid, p. 39.

the direction that "the priest is to stand so that he may with more readiness and decency break the bread before the people."

In construing an Act of Parliament, especially when penal consequences to a large number of persons depend on its construction, it would be natural if not necessary to insist upon attaching the same sense to the same expression or clause, wherever it might occur in the Act. In the eye of the law, the Prayer Book is an Act of Parliament: and we are therefore confronted by the question, how it is possible to reconcile the sense imposed upon the words " before the table " by the recent judgment of the Committee of the Privy Council, with the sense which these words have always borne, and must, from the necessity of the case, always bear, in the following Rubric in the Marriage Service :—

The Psalm ended, and the man and woman kneeling *before the Lord's Table*, the Priest standing *at* the table, and turning his face *towards* them shall say.

It is notorious that " before " is here understood to mean " on the west side of " the Holy Table, in the practice of married couples, with the sanction of bishops and clergymen, all over England. And this sense of the Rubric is in exact accordance with the direction in the Sarum book, from which it is a translation. It appears to be incompatible with the sense recently assigned to the phrase by the Judicial Committee, for reasons which are too obvious to be insisted on. But we are reminded that, for some years after the Reformation period, the tables stood in the middle of the chancel, and with the narrow

end towards the wall, so that it was possible to stand
" before " the table, and yet to " break the bread in
the sight of the people," by standing on the north
side of the table thus placed.   Yet, since the Re-
storation at least, the position of the Holy Table has
been what it is now.   Is this position, which has held
its ground almost universally during two out of the
three centuries that have passed since the Reformation, to be violently changed, in order to justify a
judgment of the Committee of the Privy Council ?
" Before the table," taken in connection with the
position which the Holy Table has continuously
occupied since the Primacy of Laud, can, surely in
common sense, only mean that precise position which
the Judicial Committee has recently condemned ?
On this part of the judgment the present Regius
Professor of Ecclesiastical History at Oxford has
observed as follows :

"In regard to the position of the Priest in Consecration it would
appear that the Judicial Committee attached some value to the
words of the Bishop—then only Archdeacon—Cosin, in his
Visitation Articles of 1627. He there presumes that the celebrant
will remain at the north side of the table, except when reading
the gospel, preaching, 'delivering the Sacrament, or on other
occasions of the like nature.' Does this illustrate the interpretation of 'before the table' in our Consecration Rubric ? Hardly
so; for when Cosin thus wrote, the Consecration Rubric ran
simply, 'Then the Priest, standing up, shall say as followeth.'
Not one word about 'standing before the table, ordering the
bread and wine, taking the elements into his hands before the
people.' The Rubric, as it now stands, was drawn up thirty-
our years after this archidiaconal visitation, and was apparently
written by Cosin himself. What would he mean by it ? That
is, would he mean to direct the Priest to consecrate in front of
the table ? In support of the affirmative view, we may observe
(1) that Cosin, when Canon of Durham, had been accused by a

violently puritanical brother Canon, Peter Smart, in 1630, of
'administering the Communion,'—a phrase which must here
mean consecrating—'with his back to the people, and his face to
the east;' and this, although the Prayer Book then in use said
nothing about 'standing before the table' (any more than about
the 'Manual Rites' in consecration, which yet, as is well known,
were generally observed, as a matter of usage, by well-instructed
Priests). And then (2) the editor of Cosin's correspondence tells
us that Cosin appears to have been in the habit of standing at the
north side except at the Consecration Prayer, which he repeated
'standing in front of the altar.' (Cosin's Correspondence, I.
p. xxvii, 199). Further (3), Cosin must have had in mind
throughout the revision of 1661, that Scottish Prayer Book of
1636, which, as the President of Magdalen well remarks, 'was
destined to exercise a material influence on the service book of
England.' (Variations of Com. and Bapt. Off., p. xxiii, 19.)
Now, that Prayer Book had a Consecration Rubric of considerable
significance; 'The Presbyter . . . . . during the time of
consecration shall stand at such a part of the Holy Table, where
he may with the more ease and decency use both his hands;' a
direction well understood by the Puritan assailants of that liturgy
to mean that the celebrant was to consecrate, not at one end of,
but in front of, a table placed—as a previous Rubric prescribed
'at the uppermost part of the chancel or church'—that is, altar-
wise—north and south, along the east wall.

"But another point deserves consideration. It has been said
that, as the Rubric about the position of the table 'in the
body of the church or chancel,' suggests a different position for
it—in fact, apparently, supposes (though certainly it does not
expressly order) the table to be set lengthways with its long sides
north and south (*See* Mr. Walton's able Pamphlet on the
'Celebrant's Position'); we cannot interpret 'before the table'
in our Consecration Rubric, as necessarily meaning 'in front of
it;' but the revisers of 1661, who framed this latter Rubric, were
thinking of a table set, as was then the case, altar-wise, along or
in front of the east wall. This arrangement, the great 'Ritual-
istic Innovation' of Charles the First's time, had made good its
ground; it was established in practice though not enjoined by
law; and to 'stand before' a table thus placed, is to stand either,
if there be room, behind it, in the old Basilican manner, or else
in front of its western side.

"But the words 'before the people' have often been supposed to forbid the Priest to consecrate in this position. An illustration, however, of the true meaning of this phrase may be derived from a somewhat similar phrase in the Coronation Office. After certain promises have been made by the sovereign, she goes to the altar steps, and there kneeling, touches the Bible held out to her by the Archbishop. Here she is evidently looking away from the people, and looking towards the altar. Yet, she is said by the Rubric to be then making 'her solemn oath *in the sight of all the people.*'" ("Maskell, Mon. Rit.," iii. 105.)[1]

If the Judicial Committee had distinctly claimed to be inspired or infallible, it would be more than indecorous in any, who admitted such a claim, to criticise its arguments. But it makes no such claim for itself, although some writers, who generally reject other inspirations and infallibilities, seem disposed to make one for it. If the Committee does not merely announce its decisions, but condescends to argue in their favour, we must presume that it invites honest criticism. We have, indeed, lately been told by the more passionate advocates of the recent judgment, that such criticism is inconsistent with the duties of a good citizen; but the substance of your letter proves that you, at least, do not assent to a doctrine which would be more consistent in an Ultramontane Bishop, enforcing "interior assent" to the decisions of the Vatican. And criticism must pronounce that the materials before the Court have been subjected to a somewhat violent process in order to make them yield the result which popular Puritanism demands. It is inconceivable, that if any but a theological interest had been at stake, any English Court could have pronounced a penal condemnation on Mr.

[1] Letter to the *Guardian.*

Purchas for " standing before the Holy Table "
during the Prayer of Consecration.

You seem to imply, and it is not for me to deny,
that in all other respects the judgment is in accordance with the Law ; but there is one other point at
least which it is difficult to pass over in silence.
Mr. Purchas is condemned for mixing water with the
wine used in celebrating the Holy Communion. The
Dean of the Arches had decided that it was illegal to
mix water with the wine at the time of the service of
the Holy Communion ; but he ruled also that this
mixture might be permitted, if it was not made at
the time of the celebration. Their Lordships dis-
allow even this scanty concession to the feeling of
every Christian scholar who knows anything of the
practice of Primitive Christendom : Bishop Horsley
practised the condemned mixture without offence, in
days when there was as yet no organized "Association" for the suppression of primitive usages.[1] But
their Lordships endeavour to reconcile Churchmen to
their decision by observing that, whilst the act of
mingling water with the wine in the Communion
Service has prevailed in the East and the West, and
is of great antiquity, the " private mingling " has
not prevailed at all. On this point Professor Bright
remarks that :—

" Not the least distressing feature in the recent judgment in the
Purchas case is the prohibition of any, even the most unobtrusive,
observance of that most venerable usage, the mixture of water
with the wine prepared for the Holy Eucharist. There is no

---

[1] Of this I have the highest presumptive evidence in a letter
from the Rev. G. Horsley Palmer.

nced to cite the testimony of St. Justin Martyr, or other ancient testimonies on this point. It is, as many will feel, a grievance that the clergy of a church which professes to follow primitive antiquity should be forbidden—as far as the present Court of Appeal can forbid them—to observe in any way whatever a Eucharistic custom, probably Apostolic, and, at any rate, as old as the first half of the second century. Granting that the public mixing of water with the wine at the time of the Offertory was to be treated as illegal; why should the private mixing, done in the vestry before service, be thus rigorously disallowed? Their lordships, we all know, had not the advantage of hearing counsel for the side against which they pronounced. Had it been otherwise, they would hardly have been left to think that the private mixture was 'not likely, in default of the public to find favour with any' or that, in fact, 'it had not prevailed at all.' It has *only* prevailed in the whole Eastern Church, as is plain from the Preparation Office, said in the side chapel of the Prothesis before the Liturgy begins; as it did prevail at low celebrations in the mediæval English Church, according to the use of Sarum. 'When Low Masses first began,' says the learned editor of the *Sarum Missal in English*, p. xliv, ' the priest was in the habit of putting the wine and water here (in the sacristy) before mass.' "[1]

Of the three points in the judgment to which I have referred, the last, probably, is the most direct contravention of that profession of conformity to the practice of the Primitive Church of Christ, which is and has always been made in the face of the world by the Reformed Church of England. The first, as you have pointed out, is the least reconcilable with the actual law of the Church and Realm; while the ruling as to the position of the celebrating Priest, in the Service for the Holy Communion, is the most calculated to cause perplexity, and in some cases more than perplexity, to a large number of the English clergy. Certainly the last point would seem to be practically of

[1] Letter to the *Guardian* of March 8, 1871.

the greatest importance : it is, by widespread consent, in the popular apprehension, more closely connected than the other two with the maintenance of Eucharistic truth. Of course, a great many epigrams may be easily composed respecting the absurdity of connecting any particular posture of a Christian, minister with the representative character of his ministerial work. In the same way, much may be and has been said about the folly of supposing that a bodily posture, like kneeling, has anything really to do with that internal homage of the soul, which is of the essence of prayer. Yet we know that, in the long run and on the whole, men who never kneel do not often pray ; and that, practically, between kneeling and prayer,—such is the relation that subsists between our souls and bodies,—the connection is so intimate that it cannot be ignored with spiritual impunity. The Sacrament of Divine Love is indeed complete wherever there is an apostolically-ordained Presbyter who will claim Christ's unfailing promise by blessing a little bread and wine, with Christ's own creative words of Institution ; whatever be the dress, or posture of the man ; whatever the shape or position of the altar or table at which he ministers ; whatever the scene in which that most real transaction—for such it is—between earth and heaven, may take place. Yet this would not justify us in insisting that the bare Eucharistic action should be stripped of all accessories, whether liturgical or ceremonial ; and thus the question is really one of degree, to be regulated by considerations of spiritual expediency. And here it is natural to think that, notwithstanding some amusing

C

paradoxes which the Dean of Westminster has advanced, the prevailing practice of Christendom, ancient and modern, may be allowed to decide that the eastward position of the Celebrant is the most convenient, as well as the most full of reverent meaning. Whether that position is, as you hold, according to the rubrics, a fairly open question, will now, perhaps, be reconsidered by the Court ; but if the Court should reconsider any part of its decision, it would, I presume, be least able to re-affirm that in which you hold it to have most clearly made a mistake ;—its decision, I mean, as to the Ornaments Rubric.

When I observed that " it was difficult to believe that the Judicial Committee was incapable of regarding the documents before it in the light of a plastic material, which might be made to support conclusions held to be advisable at the moment, and on independent grounds," I certainly did not mean to impute any dishonourable conduct to the Judges. Any such insinuation would have been absurd on the face of it, and I claim no credit for not having been guilty of what the world would have deemed a blunder as well as a crime.   But I did suppose, and meant to suggest, that the Judges looked upon themselves as entitled to exercise a discretion, which is more properly an attribute of the makers than of the administrators of the law.   No one would imagine this to hold good in the case of any other English Court of Justice; but the anomalous circumstances of the Church appeared to yield an explanation of the apparent exception.   The Church of England is a living body, the vitality, indeed, of which has been exceptionally vigorous of late years, but which, it is held, must be governed, at all hazards, without a legislature. In this land of free institutions, the Church alone is not self-governing; her convocations " contribute something to the formation of opinion ; " but we know how almost every attempt at legislative action on the part of these bodies is practically and jealously forbidden. There is, for reasons on which I do not dwell, a bright side to this state of things; Provincial Synods have no Divine warrant of inerrancy, and on more occasions than one a Convocation, free to legislate, might have cost us dear. But such a situation might go far to explain, if it does not justify, the assumption of quasi-legislative powers by the Judicial Committee. At least, whether I am right or wrong, I certainly meant to impute no sort of " dishonesty " to members of the Committee for taking a view of their duties which such circumstances would make sufficiently natural ; and persons of very high authority, who look at these matters from an altogether different point of view from any that I could adopt, agree in this estimate of the functions of the Court. " It is a Court," said the Bishop of Manchester the other day, " composed of men who look at things, not merely with the eyes of lawyers, but also with the eyes of statesmen."[1] In other words, it is a Court which exercises something like a legislative as well as a judicial control over the questions before it.[2]

---

[1] Quoted, *Guardian*, April 5, 1871.
[2] Compare the quotations in the Postscript to this Letter, pp. 50, 51.

Indeed, this theory of the action of the Court has been so commonly accepted among those to whom I have been accustomed, ever since I took Orders, nineteen years ago, to look with the greatest respect, that I was surprised at the somewhat intemperate vehemence with which it has recently been contradicted by eminent promoters of the recent prosecutions. If the functions of the Court are indeed exclusively judicial, it is not easy to justify such decisions as that in the Gorham case. The singular process by which the plain words of the Prayer Book, " Seeing now that this child is regenerate," were made to bear the now legal sense of " We hope that this child may possibly be regenerate," is unintelligible as a matter of interpretation of language; but it is not unintelligible if the Court was anxious to keep the Low Church party within the pale of the Established Church, and was authoritatively imposing a somewhat unnatural sense upon the Sacramental language of the Prayer Book in order to do so. The decision in the "Essays and Reviews " case appeared to be justifiable only on the same kind of grounds, and for reasons which Dr. Pusey pointed out at the time. So on the recent occasion, it was natural to surmise that, if the Court conceived itself to have a legislative discretion, the contradictory constructions of the Rubric before the Consecration Prayer, by which Mr. Mackonochie and Mr. Purchas were successively condemned, admitted of an explanation. This explanation necessarily exposes the Court to the inconveniences which must attend a confusion of legislative with judicial functions, but it is strictly reconcilable with the entire good faith of judges who had the interests of the Church of England, as they understood those interests, throughout in view. But if you assure me that the Judges take no such view of their duties, I must of course bow unreservedly to your authority ; although at the cost of new difficulties in explaining to myself their proceedings as critics who mean only to " ascertain " and " interpret " the law, and who disavow all wish to provide for the interests of the Church by decisions which are not forced upon them by the obvious construction of the letter of the documents which they have to interpret.

That many of the clergy intend to offer a passive resistance to the judgment is more than probable. If it is difficult to urge men to face difficulties which may be greater than others can share or understand, still less possible is it to condemn those who do face them. When you characterize such conduct as " disobedience to the Law," you appeal to a consideration, the force of which every subject of the Crown, and especially every clergyman, is bound to keep well in view. But the legal decision of a disputed archæological question is not itself any part of absolute morality, and there are occasions on which, without any factious intent, the law is tacitly ignored. The " Ecclesiastical Titles Bill " has been, unhappily, we may think, from the date of its enactment, so entirely without effect, that it is now proposed to repeal it. Another Act of Parliament does not prevent, although it ought to prevent, general smoking in railway carriages. Here the legislation of opinion, whether rightly or wrongly, amends the legislation of Parliament itself; and the result is recognized without imputations of factiousness or disloyalty. The " passive resistance " of the clergy to this Judgment means in some cases that they will not obey it unless it is enforced; in others, that if it is enforced they will take the consequences of disobedience. In favour of the first of these resolutions it may be urged that a clergyman is supposed to learn his duty, not from the reports of judicial decisions which appear in the public prints, but from his Bishop. In favour of the second, there is, I would respectfully submit, more to be said than you are willing to allow. Of course, if a Civil Court dealing with religious matters wielded an authority which could claim Divine sanction, there would be an end of all discussion. Of that more presently: but the " resisting " clergy do not recognize in this Court any authority which makes unhesitating obedience a matter of duty. In deciding whether to obey or not, they are thrown back upon the question of the spiritual expediency of obedience in a particular case. Or rather they have to balance against each other two opposing expediencies; the expediency of not giving an example of resistance to the law (I do not undervalue this), and the expediency of not undoing the work of years, of not alienating the most devoted members of their flocks, of not abandoning to Rome, or—far worse—to indifference, souls which, as it has been said, " are more precious to a good man than the safety of the Establishment." For this Judgment, if obeyed, will simply revolutionize, in many a Church, the whole character of its most solemn Service. It will involve the abandonment of usages which, in the minds of many most devout Christians, are the very outworks of inward reverence. To many who do not think accurately, or who are perhaps too much dependent upon those aids to faith which, in God's good providence, are furnished through the avenues of imagination and of sense, obedience to this judgment will appear to involve nothing less than a repudiation of portions of the revealed doctrine of the Eucharist. It is no answer to say that such inferences will be irrational. The clergy have not to deal with ideal reason ; but with average human minds as they actually are. And it will be felt by thousands that a changed service means something more than an outward change—something much more serious.

How is a clergyman to justify this sudden revolution to his people ? Is he to say, I obey the Bishop ? But is it really the Bishop who imposes the order ? Would any considerable number of the Bishops impose it, if they were taking counsel only for the good of the Church ? No ; behind the Bishop, there rises the form of the Judicial Committee. The Bishop is not here acting as a chief pastor of souls, freely dealing with his vast responsibilities ; he is reduced to the position of a legal officer ; and his moral dignity is overshadowed by the Civil Court, whose behests he obeys. One of the many mischiefs entailed upon us by the existing Court of Appeal is that it has done so much to impair the already enfeebled moral authority of our Fathers in Christ. But if they should enforce this Judgment, they must, we may be sure, enforce it upon a principle. The judgment only forms a part, on any supposition, of the whole Rubrical Law of the Church; and the Bishops must enforce the whole Rubrical Law of the Church or no part of it. The recent decision of the Final Court, if confirmed by the Queen, is not "law" in any sense in which the duty of administering the Holy Sacrament, with a separate repetition of the words of Administration, to each communicant, is not "law." Do the Bishops mean to enforce the "law" in this respect upon the Low Church Clergy? It is a parallel case. If the vestments and the eastward position of the celebrant give pain and distress to one set of communicants, the off-handed irreverence of "railful administrations," as they are termed, gives at least an equal amount of pain to another set. They see in it, and surely not quite without reason, a very significant symbolism— the symbolism of a persistent depreciation of the Sacraments of Christ.[1] In those precious moments, unlike any others that are passed on earth, when the soul meets its Maker and its Redeemer in the intimate embrace of an ineffable communion, the perfunctory officialism which seems to say, "The sooner we get this all over the better," is a source of sharp pain to reverent and believing minds. Others I know have felt it; I myself have felt it; and compared with this pain, I should think, any annoyance caused by differences of dress, or differences of posture, to those who too often do not suppose them-

---

[1] I have myself heard an "Evangelical" preacher refer to the Sacraments as "wood, hay, and stubble," in the pulpit.

selves to be doing anything more serious than taking
a little bread and wine in public, in memory of an
absent Christ, would be very endurable indeed.

There is a question which it is not, I trust, disrespectful to ask, since it cannot, in justice, be ignored
in this connection. Is it not the case that, since this
judgment has been delivered, at the recent Royal
Marriage, the Service prescribed in the Book of
Common Prayer was largely mutilated by the officiating bishop or bishops ? Is not the Marriage Service
part of an Act of Parliament, and could its mutilation
be legally authorized without the consent of Parliament ? It is easy to understand the difficulty in which
the bishops may have been placed ; probably any one
else in their circumstances, considering the *jus litur-
gicum* inherent in the Episcopate, would have acted
as they did. But this does not alter the fact that
they broke the " law ; " as indeed they break it on
other occasions, which it would be as unwelcome as
it is needless to specify. Can they then, with a good
conscience, admonish, suspend, deprive their clergy
for doing that which they have done, either actually
or by connivance, themselves ? A higher than any
living bishop has, in another connection, written
words which appeal to the profoundest instincts of
our common human conscience, and which must, I
feel sure, stay the hand and silence the voice of more
than one of our Fathers in God. It was to the typi-
cal Jew, making his boast in the Mosaic law, that
St. Paul preached a doctrine of justice which is,
historically speaking, older and broader than that
Gospel which is based on it : " Wherein thou judgest

another, thou condemnest thyself; for thou that judgest doest the same things. . . . . Thou, therefore, which teachest another, teachest thou not thyself? Thou that preachest a man should not steal, dost thou steal? Thou that sayest a man should not commit adultery, dost thou commit adultery? Thou that abhorrest idols, dost thou commit sacrilege?"[1]

The Archbishop of Canterbury, indeed, when recently anticipating his answer to the Clergy who were still signing the remonstrance against the recent judgment, hastens to relieve the anxieties of the remonstrants in the following terms:—

"You fear lest the liberty of the clergy may be unduly interfered with, and you deprecate the evil which might arise from the sudden introduction in many parishes of changes from practices which you believe have given no offence, and which have been adopted under the conscientious conviction that they were not irreconcilable with the law. I will not, therefore, hesitate to remind you that the whole practice of the Episcopate of England in the administration of its duties, is averse to anything like tyrannical interference with individual liberty. We have long learned by experience that we can trust our clergy; and, except when complaints are made against their mode of performing divine service, our rule is to leave them to act according to their own consciences, under direction of the Rubrics.

"I have already intimated to others that what I conceive this judgment has done is, to state the law in reference to the illegality of the so-called sacrificial vestments, and in reference to the position of the officiating minister at the celebration of the Holy Communion. The Rubrics, interpreted by the Supreme Court, form the lawful rule of divine service, to which the clergy are bound to yield a loyal obedience, and of which they are bound to observe every particular when required by authority. But certainly, as a matter of fact, not all the clergy are expected

---

[1] Rom. ii. 1, 21, 22.

by their parishioners, or required by their Bishops, rigidly to observe every point in the Rubrics at all times and under all circumstances.

"No doubt in such matters the clergy will be ready to listen to the paternal advice of their Bishops, which, I feel sure, will always be given with full consideration of the particular circumstances of our parishes, and of the delicacy and difficulty of introducing changes from established usage. Still, in points where the law is clear, the chief officers of the Church must of course be prepared to enforce its observance in cases which are brought before them in a legal way."[1]

When his Grace observes that, "as a matter of fact, *not all* the Clergy are expected by their parishioners, or required by their Bishops, rigidly to observe every point in the Rubrics at all times and under all circumstances," he is keeping within the truth, since the statement probably applies to nine-tenths of the Clergy of the Church of England. It is applicable in a very emphatic sense to the Low Church party, as every one knows who attends their ministrations and is moderately acquainted with the Prayer Book and its Rubrics. There is no intention on the part of the Episcopate to enforce literal obedience to the Rubric on the Low Church Clergy. The great mistake of the surplice crusade of 1844 is not likely to be repeated. The Primate, with his eye on this grave fact, is too equitable to use the language which alone would satisfy a section of the Puritan and anti-religious press. He appears to imply that the Bishops will not, of their own motion, enforce the judgment. But they will enforce it "in cases which are brought before them in a legal way." It is, therefore, of the utmost practical importance to

[1] *Daily News*, April 12, 1871.

ask whether they will be pressed to enforce the judgment; and on this point we have, I regret to say, no reason for entertaining a doubt.

On Wednesday, March 1st, the Church Association held its sixth annual meeting in St. James's Hall, and a full report of its proceedings appeared in the *Record* of Friday, March 3rd. The attendance was very large; and, after a great party triumph, it was natural that there should be an interchange of warm congratulations, and that the tone of the meeting should be jubilant. If the only object of the Church Association had been, as is sometimes asserted, to "ascertain the law" by a course of litigation, it would have been natural to say to the defeated party, "We have vindicated our opinion as to the legal sense of the formularies of the Church of England; and, having done this, we are glad to let a distressing controversy drop as quietly and as entirely as may be." But in a leading article the *Record* informs us that :—

"The key-note was sounded in the excellent opening address of the Vice-chairman of the Council, and the tone of mingled thankfulness for the past (more especially for the Purchas judgment), and firm adherence to principle in view of the future, characterized the remaining proceedings."[1]

Turning then to the speech of the chairman, I find him using very distinct language, and I italicise the sentences which appear to me to have most practical significance of a serious character. He thinks that the Judgment will generally be obeyed, but then he proceeds to say that :—

---

[1] *Record*, March 3, 1871.

" Where there is disobedience we must remit these men to the kind consideration of the Bishops. (Hear, hear.) It will ill become me to say one word against the Bishops. They have been very cautious. (Hear, hear.) They perhaps have had some colour for their non-action; but at least they have not been in haste to mark these men as offenders. But whatever justification they had, were it as flimsy as a cobweb, that is now put on one side, and no ingenuity can now justify non-action on the part of the Bishops. (Cheers.) The name of the Bishop of London is mentioned in the Report, and I think too good of his Lordship to say that he has any sympathy at all with Ritualism or Ritualists. (Hear, hear.) I believe him to be a perfectly sincere and conscientious man. I have no doubt that he is a cautious man, that he is a man who likes peace. He is placed so as to preside over a Church that is comprehensive, and we cannot blame him for being cautious. But I believe that now the law is defined the Bishop of London will be as firm in enforcing obedience to that law as he has been pertinacious hitherto in not taking any active measures. (Hear, hear.) But while endeavouring to place a load on the Bishops' shoulders, let us not forget that we ourselves have *a duty* to perform. The law is so clearly defined now that we can have no doubt about it; and *the Church Association intend to embody in a handy-book the late judgment, so that no man or woman can plead ignorance as to what is the law and what is not the law.* (Cheers.) It is our duty as members of the Church of England to see that the law is obeyed. Let not the Bishops have this excuse, 'We have no complaints.' When there is a violation of the law, let there be an abundance of complaints. (Cheers.) Do you, the laity of the Church of England, be faithful, *be vigilant, be unsparing.* Be not petulant, hasty, or equivocal; but wherever there is a clear infraction of this authoritative decision, *let the Bishop have no peace until he interferes.* (Loud and repeated cheers.) I am old enough to remember that that arch-agitator, Mr. O'Connell, used the words "Agitate, agitate, agitate." Well, now, the children of this world are in their generation wiser than the children of light. Do you take a leaf out of his book, and you may depend upon this, that a faithful laity will make a vigilant clergy."[1]

The Rev. J. C. Ryle appears to follow in the same sense :—

[1] Speech of Mr. T. R. Andrews, *Record*, March 3, 1871.

" We have been warned about what Ritualists may do, but I should like to know what the Bishops intend to do. What has recently passed in the Upper House in Convocation makes me not only desire that Convocation may be reformed root and branch, but that in the meantime the members might have a muzzle put on their lips. After what took place the other day in the Upper House of Convocation, I feel rather shy in speaking about the Bishops, but, nevertheless, I hope the Bishops will not forget that the law has now been made clear, plain, and definite on the points upon which Mr. Purchas has been prosecuted. (Hear, hear.) The Bishops will no longer plead uncertainty. (Hear, hear.) They can no longer plead that these questions are not settled by law: they can no longer hide themselves, as it were, in a jungle, and say that these matters are left without legal decision. (Cheers.) There is a legal decision; the law has been plainly laid down; and now what the Bishops will be expected to do may be summed up in an application of the words of the immortal Nelson on the day of Trafalgar. The Church of England will expect the Bishops to "do their duty." (Loud cheers.)—*Record*, March 3, 1871.

Had the chairman's remarks been unwelcome to the meeting, it might have been expected that the Dean of Carlisle, as the only dignitary of the Church who was present on the occasion, would have softened or explained them. But the Dean opened his speech by saying :—

" I always think it very pleasant and anticipate much satisfaction from being well abused by enemies, because I get equally well applauded by friends, and that comforts me on the other side. (Hear, and laughter.) I have been invited to come here and support the good cause, and what I have heard has given me the greatest satisfaction. I have loved this institution from its very commencement. I have watched its progress, and, so far as I know and believe, I approve of everything that it has done. (Cheers.) I have been surprised from time to time at the great wisdom with which its affairs have been conducted."—*Record*, March 3, 1871.

The Dean is not without hope that, in a still

graver case which must come before it, the Judicial
Committee will prove itself equally satisfactory to
the Church Association :—

" There is one point which has not been alluded to in the
important judgment which has recently been given. That judgment is not a declaration merely against the use of certain dresses
in the Church, but there is a distinct reference to them as being
unlawful because they are sacrificial. I have read the judgment
carefully several times, and find that the Committee of Council
has decided against all these things because they represent
' sacrificing priests.' Having adopted that principle in regard to
vestments, they cannot go from it when they give their next
judgment on doctrine in the case of Mr. Bennett, and therefore
ere long I anticipate the final result of your labours in that case."
(Cheers.)—*Record*, March 3, 1871.

The meeting was naturally enthusiastic in its
praises of the Judicial Committee, but its enthusiasm
was not extended to any of our existing Church Courts.
The Court of Arches, in particular, had not deserved
well of the Association, and the Dean alludes to it in
terms which I do not call " disloyal," whatever else
may or may not be rightly said of them :—

" Perhaps you are not all aware what is the nature of the
Ecclesiastical Courts. First of all, there is your own beloved
Court of Arches here in London. The Report tells us that " the
mode of procedure in the Ecclesiastical Courts has long been felt
to be cumbrous, dilatory, and expensive." There could not be a
better description of them than that. These old Courts are in the
present day quite out of date. It is just as if any one were to
bring out the arquebusses and blunderbusses of former times and
pit them against the French chassepôts and the Prussian needle-
guns. (Laughter.) These Courts are quite out of keeping with
the times ; they won't go off, they won't move, they are of no
use ; while, as regards expense, we have spent £18,000 in carry-
ing on our proceedings. It is high time that those Courts
reformed their ways. (Hear, hear.) This Court of Arches—
(" Dark Arches," and laughter)—yes, Gothic arches of the middle

ages (laughter)—this Court is, I say, called, humorously enough, 'the Court below,' I suppose because its judgments are generally set aside by the Court above. (Great laughter.) But this is only one of those antiquated places. There are other Courts of a similar nature all over the country. In every diocese there is what is called a Consistory Court, which is very much like the Court of Arches, and which serves in the provinces very much the same purpose as that Court serves here."—*Record*, March 3, 1871.

There is in the speech of Canon Hoare an expression of pain at being " compelled by a strong sense of duty to embark in such a conflict." This note of Christian feeling is not quite in harmony with the general tone of the meeting : but the practical result is not affected by it. It is plain that the chairman's advice will be acted on, and that the system of *espionage* and organized terrorism, which has been brought to bear on some churches in London, will be extended throughout the country. Indeed, I am told that this is already the case in some parishes in the West of England. The most solemn service of the Church is attended, not for purposes of prayer and devotion, but in order to mark any " illegal " peculiarities in the officiating clergyman that can be used with a view to persecuting him. And had the late judgment been confirmed by Her Majesty, there can be no doubt that we should have had some very practical illustrations of the full meaning of the chairman's advice.

It is in the light of this meeting, and, I may add, of the article in which the leading journal introduced the judgment to the attention of the country, that the Archbishop's language must be read. The writer of that article, when referring to the one great theological school which the Church of England has produced since the Reformation, spoke significantly enough of "the comparatively darkened days of Caroline divinity." The Archbishop is, as every one knows, a sincerely tolerant man ; but the fact remains that he will be forced to persecute at the bidding of Puritanism. Yet we are no longer living in the seventeenth century : and the Church Association may discover that its victory will turn out to be nothing less than a serious disaster to some of the interests it professes to have at heart. It will have succeeded, if it does succeed in its programme, in straining existing institutions to a point which is incompatible with the safety of the Church Establishment.

It is indeed a serious source of weakness to our Church at this moment, that we have a Supreme Court which fails to touch the conscience of a large body of the clergy. Its particular decisions may or may not be welcome to them ; but they do not command that hearty assent which would greet them if they emanated from an unquestioned authority. The constitution of the Court is, of itself, fatal to its moral empire : its real power is commensurate with the penalties it can inflict. The reasons for this are independent of the character of any particular judges who may sit to hear Ecclesiastical appeals : even the high integrity of Lord Hatherley, and the transparently sincere piety and equitable moderation of the present Bishop of London, cannot neutralize the force of a bad tradition. Could such a Troy have been saved by any men, these would assuredly have

saved it. But Mr. Joyce has pointed out in his
learned and exhaustive work, " The Civil Power in its
Relations to the Church," the nature and number of
the reasons which for many years past have made
this Court a rock of offence to intelligent and earnest
Churchmen. Among these the origin of the Court is
conspicuous ; the Court is the product of a legislative
blunder. By the statute 3 and 4 William IV. 41,
a Court was formed of members of the Privy Council for the purpose of hearing appeals in Admiralty
and Colonial causes. Among the subordinate Courts
which were meant to be affected by the statute, there
is no mention of any Ecclesiastical Court whatever ;
and Lord Brougham, the chief author of the Act,
stated in the House of Lords that " he could not
help feeling that the Judicial Committee of the Privy
Council had been framed without the expectation of
[Ecclesiastical] questions . . . . being brought before
it. It was created for the consideration of a totally
different class of cases, and he had no doubt but
that if it had been constituted with a view to such
cases as the present [the Gorham case] , some other
arrangement would have been made."[1] In the same
way Bishop Blomfield asserted that, when this tribunal was created " the contingency of a doctrinal
appeal came into no one's mind."[2]   Bishop Blomfield had been a member of the Commissions of
1831 and 1832, which reported that " the Privy
Council being composed of Lords temporal and
spiritual, &c. . . . . seems to comprise the materials

[1] Hans. 3 s., vol. cxi., p. 629, quoted by Joyce.
[2] Hans. 3 s., vol. cxi., p. 600, quoted by Joyce.

of a most perfect tribunal for deciding appeals from the Ecclesiastical Courts"; but Bishop Blomfield knew that although the presence of "Lords Spiritual" in the Privy Council was a main reason for the recommendation of the commissioners, no single spiritual person was appointed a member of the Court by the Act 3 and 4 William IV. 41.

Mr. Joyce attributes the mistake, by which Ecclesiastical appeals were referred to the Judicial Committee of the Privy Council as constituted in 1833, to the profuse verbiage indulged in by the draftsman·of the statute. He "permitted himself, in the commencement of a section in which he was about to provide for appeals then pending and unheard, to launch out into some wide and undistinguishing language, which, unintentionally, so far as the Legislature was concerned, involved Ecclesiastical causes in their too ample embraces. And though no hint of any Ecclesiastical Court or cause whatsoever occurs throughout all the enacting clauses of this statute," yet this rhetorical exuberance has, in fact, entailed upon us "the evil, which the Church of England has never since ceased to deplore."[1]

On this point, as I regret to think, your great authority is opposed to a reform which Mr. Keble believed to be nothing less than essential to the wellbeing and safety of the Church. He believed, as you say, that the successors of the Apostles were, according to the mind of our Lord, the proper persons to decide questions of Christian doctrine in the Church of Christ. This was a natural corollary of

[1] Joyce, "The Civil Power," &c., p. 80. *See* the whole chapter.

his belief that our Lord had expressly instituted an order of men, charged with the duty of teaching and guarding the faith, that they might feed and guide His own flock to the end of time. It was useless, Mr. Keble used to argue, to exclude unauthorized teachers from the pulpit, if you admitted unauthorized teachers to decide what might or might not be taught from the pulpit. The argument for an ordained order of teachers—the argument which is admitted and advanced by all Christian bodies except Independents, Quakers, and Plymouth Brethren—is the argument which is fatal to the decision of doctrinal questions, or of questions which affect the integrity of Christian doctrine, even indirectly, by the Judicial Committee.

The Judicial Committee is really a Civil Court, framed for the purpose of hearing Admiralty and Colonial appeals. The presiding judges may or may not believe in Christianity; but, under the form of "ascertaining" the law by interpreting legal documents, which are also Church formularies, they do, as a matter of fact, undertake to decide the very weightiest questions of Christian doctrine. Certainly the two Primates and the Bishop of London may sit to hear Ecclesiastical appeals. But the "Essays and Reviews" judgment showed for how little the authority of our highest Prelates counts, when it is opposed to the opinion of the lay judges. The Bishops really serve only to decorate a machine which is worked by lay hands; they throw a delusive sanction of religious authority over the decisions of the Civil Court, and thus enable inaccurate writers and speakers to term it a final Church Court. Their presence has little real effect beyond that of creating widespread embarrassment and distress in consciences when the Court decides against the necessity of fundamental Church doctrine ; or against the lawfulness of what has hitherto been permitted in Church belief or Church practice.

Certainly, it would seem to be most consistent with faith in our Lord's precepts and promises to make the entire Episcopate of England and Wales a Court of final appeal in questions of doctrine and discipline. The Queen would still judge spiritual causes, but through the Spiritualty ; and the Bishops would, doubtless, be assisted by legal advisers, to prevent collisions with the civil law. When you ask whether such a Court might not pronounce unsatisfactory judgments, I do not forget that the Bishops of a single province, or of two provinces, cannot claim an unerring guidance into truth ; and that an episcopate appointed by statesmen, all of whom cannot be always supposed to have the spiritual interests of the Church entirely at heart, is likely from time to time to include persons who unhappily do not possess the confidence of the Church in their capacity of guardians of the Faith. But, in the long run, what the world would call the ecclesiastical instinct—what I should term a conscientious recognition of the first duty of ministers of Christ—would probably prove a sufficient guarantee. The Bishops would judge in such a Court under a sense of responsibility, which it is impossible that they should feel as members of a Convocation which cannot alter a single Canon without a Royal licence. The Lambeth Synod of 1867 has taught us, amid much else, how much reason there is for trusting the Chief Pastors of the Church, even against appearances, when they are fairly thrown back upon their spiritual instincts, and forced to face their heaviest spiritual responsibilities. And, if the episcopal judges in this Court had, each of them, to give his reasons for his decision, in writing, we should possess an additional reason for believing that the Court would decide theological questions, not entirely without respect to theological as well as to legal principles, and that with such a tribunal some, at any rate, of our difficulties in late years might have been avoided.

But it is useless to discuss the impracticable; and every one seems to agree that a Church Court of Appeal is out of the question in the present temper of public opinion. If this be so, we should escape from much spiritual distress, could the present Court be entirely stripped of its useless ecclesiastical fringe, and be made in appearance what it is in reality— a Civil Court. A purely Civil Court would only deal with Church questions, as questions touching the tenure of property and personal rights. Its decisions might entail serious pecuniary inconvenience in particular cases. But it would not wound and harass consciences; it would not give itself the airs, or be invested by popular misapprehension with the prerogatives of the Vatican. It would not pronounce any purely spiritual sentences; such as was the suspension of Mr. Mackonochie *à sacris,* without any reference to the Bishop of the Diocese, last autumn. The practical effect

would be to put us very much on the same footing
as all other religious bodies in the country, in this
respect : and we should escape from the threatening
evil of an ever-accumulating body of disciplinary and
doctrinal decisions, emanating from a Court which
was constructed for the purpose of hearing appeals in
Admiralty and Colonial cases.

That this Court is a source of real danger to
the security of the Establishment appears to me
to be beyond doubt. It enlists on behalf of some
fundamental change in our relations with the State,
the very hearts and consciences which, under happier
circumstances, would be most averse to such a
change. Decision after decision has given a shock
to the old conviction that we cannot pay too dearly
for the many blessings of a Church Establishment :
and this has led to language which would have been
impossible twenty years ago. There are, of course,
persons to whom the Church of our Divine Redeemer is only so much income and so much position ; and the forfeiture of these things is, in their
eyes, the forfeiture of everything. They talked
quite consistently, two years ago, of the "destruc-
tion" and of the "abolition" of the Irish Church.
But to those whose loyalty to the Church of God is
entirely independent of the accident of her "Establishment," and who love her as well in her disesta-
blished poverty in Scotland as they love her in her
English splendour, the question presents itself in a
different light. Nor can I at all endorse language
which has of late been applied apparently to all
the advocates of disestablishment outside the Church.

I cannot think that a man who advocates disestablishment is necessarily an enemy of Almighty God, although, possibly enough, some of His enemies may advocate it. Probably I have much less in common with the imperfect faith, as I must deem it, of eminent Nonconformists, such as Mr. Dale, or Mr. Spurgeon, than some writers who have used what appears to me to be very violent language about the advocates of disestablishment; but it never would occur to me to describe either of the above-named gentlemen as an enemy of God. Surely a man might desire the disestablishment of the Church from the purest and loftiest motives, such as a real wish to advance the interests of pure religion as he understands them. I am very far from saying that such means would certainly secure the end in view; but that an advocate of disestablishment is necessarily a wicked man, appears to be a paradox which is too absurd to be seriously discussed, although it is not too absurd to be sometimes assumed without discussion.

Certainly, you do me simple justice by pointing out that I do not undertake to agitate for disestablishment, and that in hazarding a conditional prediction upon the subject I sincerely disclaim the intention of uttering even an indirect menace. But I hear what is said freely around me, not by our opponents, not by dissenters from the Church, but by some of her most devoted sons, by clergy and laity alike. Of late years there has been a noticeable change of opinion among younger men, as to the balance of blessings and drawbacks which the establishment of religion involves; and for this change the existing Court of Final Appeal is mainly responsible. I entirely follow you in all that you urge in favour of Church Establishments. Apart from those grave bearings of the matter on education at this particular juncture, to which you advert, disestablishment would probably involve nothing less than the entire withdrawal of the presence of the Church's ministrations from considerable portions of the rural population; however, it might, as I believe it would in some cases, strengthen our hold upon the towns. It would occasion an unsettlement of the many national, local, social traditions, which surround and recommend religion in England, so vast and wide-spreading in itself and in its results, that the imagination recoils from the task of tracing it. And where so much resulting loss and injury to souls would be an inevitable consequence of a particular measure, few men who were free to decline the responsibility would be anxious, or other than most unwilling, to urge it forward.

But what if it be pressed upon us as our only escape from a thraldom which threatens the very existence of that which alone makes an Established Church worth upholding ? After all, position and income are worth nothing to a servant of Christ, except as means for spreading his Master's truth and his Master's kingdom, and if they can only be retained by a clerical order upon conditions which are incompatible with this supreme object, the sooner they are abandoned the better. The recent judgment would not have occasioned the deep and far-reaching uneasiness, of which we witness so many symptoms, if it had stood alone. The naturally Conservative temper of the Clergy would still have prescribed silence on the subject of our anomalous Court of Final Appeal, if the Court had not strained its authority to a point which the most competent and respected of religious tribunals could scarcely have attempted with impunity. As it is, after interpreting the formularies with extraordinary laxity—to use no stronger expression—in order to retain the .Evangelical and Latitudinarian parties within the Established Church, the Court now imposes upon them a narrowing interpretation, which you do not attempt to defend, and by which High Churchmen are to be offered the alternative of abandoning their historical traditions or being excluded from the Ministry. The natural result is a wide-spread feeling that justice is not to be expected from the Final Court; and, among other lamentable consequences, this feeling has already had the effect of depriving the Church of the services of young men of great promise, who have abandoned their intention of becoming candidates for Orders. Sound Churchmen, they are convinced, must not expect toleration from the Final Court which rules us; and this sense of injustice, if I except the section of political Churchmen with whom secular interests are really stronger than religious ones, is very general. It is unnecessary to say that such a feeling is a very powerful lever, and that, again and again, it has been among the most formidable enemies of institutions which uphold or acquiesce in that which provokes it. Not that this is the only, or by any means the chief, reason of danger to the Establishment. Religious men do not yield to the sense of personal wrong unless it is reinforced by principle. The threatened proscription of High Churchmen is the proscription of that which they teach; it is, in effect, the proscription of all that distinguishes the faith of Andrewes and of Keble from that of the Puritanism of the seventeenth century or of our own day. If the Established Church is to be committed to this proscription, its victims will naturally endeavour to secure a continuance of those spiritual and sacramental blessings which descend through an Apostolically commissioned ministry, apart from the State connection which impedes or obscures a full manifestation of Sacramental Truth.

Twenty years ago our graver difficulties would perhaps have been met in another way : we know to our cost how such perplexities were solved by some of the noblest and purest souls whom God has ever given to the Church of England. But in 1845 and 1851 the Definition of the Immaculate Conception had not yet presented the Roman Church under the eyes of this generation in the light of a dogmatic innovator; all was still as it had been left by the Council of Trent, and beyond that date much was taken for granted. Moreover, the great mind which led the Romeward movement was more intent upon noting what the Fathers of the undivided Church had taught, than upon enquiring what Western Mediævalism had added to their teaching, and how the additions had been made. Still less in those days had a majority in a Vatican Council committed the Church of Rome to doctrinal positions which, in the eyes of all educated men who are free to form an opinion on the subject, are simply irreconcilable with the facts of history. It had not yet become necessary for the Papal Court to anathematize the consummate learning and fearless honesty of the first Roman Catholic theologian of the continent, Dr. Döllinger. It was still possible to plead, as Roman Catholic prelates pleaded at the period of the Emancipation Act, that Papal Infallibility was nothing more than a permissible opinion. All this has changed, and although Rome may still attract imaginative sentiment, or wounded feeling, she has lost much of, if not all, her power over sincere but embarrassed religious thought. Nor, if it were possible and legitimate, is the Non-juring experiment of a nature to invite repetition ; and the hints which a respected Prelate is understood to have thrown out, to the effect that clergy who cannot submit to the judgment of the Committee had better be guilty of open schism, will be more likely to impair his own moral authority than to be obeyed. If the Apostolical precepts about submission to the powers that be, could apply to the case of a secular Court dealing with strictly religious interests, there would be reason for a part of this advice ; but no one imagines that St. Paul would have submitted to a decision of Nero's on the subject of Justification, or in any particular which implied one or another doctrine about it. Surely, our rulers do not intend to repeat the mistake which created Wesleyanism. They cannot really mean that schism is the only alternative to submission to the secular Court which they have in view! Is it wise to force men to stand at bay—to drive them to extremities rather than abandon the ideal of an impossible and useless uniformity? It is not for me to answer these questions ; but if they are decided in the intolerant sense, the decision will lead to grave consequences sooner or later. Sooner than leave the English Church, or allow her to be Puritanized or Rationalized beyond recall, Churchmen will at least refuse to resist, if they do not actively assist politicians who, for purposes of their own, may promise the freedom as well as the poverty of dis-establishment.

Certainly, I thankfully re-echo your words, as to the relations which might well exist between the two great and unhappily divided sections of the English Church. I wish it were possible to say that the "unsparing" animosity of which Churchmen are the object had never been provoked by any want of consideration for the lawful or mistaken preju-dices of others, and that the natural and reverent expression of great lines of faith and thought had never been caricatured by exaggeration. But Church-men should be the last to claim impeccability ; and it is grateful to remember that the Evangelical party has again and again given of its best and holiest to the High Church ranks. To Evangelicalism Church-men owe two of the instruments which enable them at this moment to do good spiritual work among the people most effectively. It would be untrue and ungrateful to deny how largely the Evangelical idea

of preaching has superseded the old essay-reading
theory which was upheld by the dry orthodoxy of
a previous day ; and, if we look to the matter as
well as the method of High Church sermons, the
personal and affectionate devotion to our Blessed
Saviour, which now pre-eminently characterizes them,
is a legacy of the Cecils and the Wilberforces rather
than of the more ecclesiastical school of the be-
ginning of the century. In Hymnody the debt to
Evangelicalism is still greater ; we never can sufficiently acknowledge the supreme service of ridding
the Church of England—and at the cost of no little
personal obloquy and inconvenience to the men
who first dared to innovate—of Tate and Brady's
Psalms. Certainly the modern Evangelical Hymn-
books are too exclusively subjective ; and on the
Sacramental side of Divine revelation they are doc-
trinally defective. But they have done a work for
the positive and fundamental truths which centre
in the Divine Person and atoning work of our
Adorable Lord, and the sanctifying power of His
Holy Spirit, to which, as I believe, Church History
will one day render a more ample justice than has
yet been done. Nor is it accurate to say that the
old fire of Evangelicalism is extinct. It produces
Biblical scholars, like Mr. Birks, whom we all read
with the deepest respect and with abundant profit,
and conscientious students of the problems which
surround the existence and claims of Revelation such
as is Mr. Garbett ; and it can point to devoted parish
priests, like Mr. Cadman, of St. Marylebone, whose
lives and works illuminate and warm many others

who only know them by report. The rude controversialists of the Church Association are, in the main, men of another moral and intellectual order; but I, at least, shall not despair of seeing an end of their deteriorating influence with a school to which we all owe not a few such debts as those I have glanced at. There is enough, God knows, in the England of to-day to make every man who thinks at all anxious about the future, and every religious man anxious for religious union. The social chasms which threaten to open beneath our feet and pour out a burning torrent of revolutionary lava, call for all the self-denying charity which a united Church can yield, while there is yet time, to heal the wounds and strengthen the bands of a diseased and divided society. The moral sores of that society are not skin-deep; and Infidelity never threatened, not Christianity merely, but Theism of any intelligible description, more seriously than it does now. It is piteous indeed that we should be wrangling over such questions as are raised by this Judgment in presence of these absorbing anxieties; but wounds are not healed by ignoring them, and I see no path of safety except in frank and mutual toleration and respect. High Churchmen, I trust, will never be guilty of endeavouring to force the Evangelical clergy into surplices which would disturb good men or offend their congregations, or into copes which would make their wearers grotesque. On the other hand, it is not yet too late for the higher minds of the Evangelical party to determine that they will discourage all attempts to enforce an oppressive Judgment,—a Judgment, which, whether it be re-heard and reversed or not, you have shown to involve a miscarriage of Justice.

Pardon me, my dear Sir John, for the crudities and the freedom of a letter which cannot, in any one respect, affect your opinion, but which may be of use, as I believe it, indeed, to be dictated by duty, on other accounts. Much as I should have preferred silence, even to this respectful acknowledgment of what you have written, I cannot altogether regret an occasion which has enabled me to forward you so careful an expression of anxious thought about the present crisis, as that which accompanies my own communication.

I am, my dear Sir John Coleridge,
With sincere respect,
Yours very faithfully,
H. P. LIDDON.

3, *Amen Court, St. Paul's,*
Easter-tide, 1871.

P.S.—I. In the words of Messrs. Brodrick and Freemantle, the results of the judgment in the "Essays and Reviews" case were "that it is allowable for a Clergyman to deny that every part of every Book of the Bible is inspired," or to speak of the Bible as "an expression of devout reason," or as "the written voice of the Congregation," or of parts of it as "dark patches of human error and passion which form a partial crust on it:" he may also express a hope of the forgiveness of the wicked after the final day of judgment, and speak of the doctrine of "merit by transfer (*i.e.*, 'the imputation of Christ's merits') as a fiction." Quoted, in *West. Rev.*, No. 78, p. 361.

In his letter to the *Times*, of March 14, 1871, the Dean of Ripon writes : " To those who will not submit to what is declared to be the law of the Church, we have a right to say, You are no longer lawfully members of the Church."

Am I then to infer that in the opinion of the Dean of Ripon and of the Evangelical party, lawful Church-membership is forfeited by teaching the inspiration of all Scripture, its inerrancy, the endlessness of future punishments, and the imputation of Christ's merits, *unless* it be immediately added that it is *legal* for a minister of the Church of England to deny every one of these tenets ?   Yet clearly a full submission " to what is now declared to be the law of the Church," would imply nothing less than this. I do not for one moment suppose that the Evangelical clergy are guilty of such thorough-going unfaithfulness to their most cherished convictions as a *complete* submission to the judgment of the Judicial Committee in the case of " Essays and Reviews " would imply. But then must they not disavow such language, as that which I quote from the Dean, in reference to another judgment of the same Court which happens to gratify their prejudices against usages which some of their brethren deem a reverent expression of the revealed doctrine of the Holy Sacrament ?

Quam temere in nosmet, legem sancimus iniquam !

II. That the theory of a quasi-legislative action on

E

the part of the Judicial Committee is not easily set aside must, I think, appear from an examination of the judgment delivered in Mr. Voysey's case. I take this case because, in matters of such overwhelming importance, my sympathies are much more strongly enlisted than in the Purchas case, and they are enlisted unreservedly on the side of the conclusion arrived at by the Court. Yet it is impossible to deny that Mr. Voysey had a right to expect greater protection from previous judgments than he actually received; and such distinctions as those recognized by the Court between denying "passages" of Scripture and denying "whole chapters" to be the Word of God, or, again, between "the private taste and judgment" of the appellant, and a judgment "on critical grounds"—such as, I suppose, that of the Essayists was held to be—can only be explained by a desire on the part of the Court to erect barriers against the logical results of a previous decision. A "chapter" is, of course, a purely artificial division of a book of Holy Scripture; and every impugner of Holy Scripture who rejected any part of it on the strength of "his own private taste and judgment" would be certain to persuade himself that he did so "on critical grounds," whatever those grounds might be really worth. Commenting on another feature of the Voysey judgment, a writer in the *Westminster Review* observes :—" We see no other way of explaining it but by *the desire and intention of the Court to reclaim the liberty incautiously conceded* to the Clergy in the case of 'Essays and Reviews.' Great lawyers have sometimes had to complain of judge-made law; the

Church seems likely to be accommodated with a good deal of judge-made theology." (No. 78, p. 369.) I cannot profess the slightest sympathy with the writer of this passage, or with the article in which it occurs : but on that very account I am the better able to appeal to it as confirmatory of an opinion which Churchmen have largely entertained for twenty years as to the real action of the Court of Final Appeal.

Another testimony, equally independent as coming from an equally disinterested observer, occurs in the current number of the *British Quarterly Review*,[1] which is understood to be edited by one of the most accomplished Congregational ministers in London. The writer does not appear to have the Purchas judgment so much in view as earlier decisions of the Final Court. Speaking of the "comprehensiveness" of the Church of England, as understood and upheld by the Broad Church party, he observes that " the aim of the " Courts has been, as far as possible, to maintain this " view, on behalf of which they have often strained " the language of the law to a dangerous extent, and, in " fact, *have allowed mere custom to set aside the authority* " *of law in a way which certainly would not have been* " *tolerated in any proceedings relative to property or civil* " *right*. The expositions of Ecclesiastical Law, as " given even by the highest Court, have often been " remarkable as illustrations of the *dexterity with which* " *the judges have rescued the Church from positions of* " *great difficulty*, rather than as examples of sound inter- " pretation of the Statutes. *Considerations of public*

---

[1] No. 106, April 1, 1871, pp. 353, 354.

" *policy have affected the decisions, and the strict letter of*
" *the law has been disregarded in a fashion which would*
" *find little favour in Westminster Hall.*   The question
" has been, not as to the positive requirements of the
' Statute, if construed on the ordinary principles of
" language, but as to the amount of latitude to be
" permitted; and so far has this been carried, that the
" defendant in a recent suit was bold enough to quote
' a passage from a letter of Dr. Arnold, which was not
" published till after his death, as illustrative of the
" liberty which had been granted to him, and which,
" therefore, though to a much greater extent, he de-
" manded for himself."

Letter

FROM THE REV. E. B. PUSEY, D.D.
TO REV. DR. LIDDON.

My Dearest Liddon,

The letter of my friend, and the early friend of him who we so much loved and reverenced, John Keble, touches on so many questions, upon which we have thought and felt in common, that I cannot but wish to supplement any letter which you may feel compelled to write to Sir J. T. Coleridge, by expressing to you what must in the main be our common thoughts.

I. In regard to the subject-matter of the Purchas judgment, I am, even less than yourself, able to make myself amenable to it; for, being a member of a Chapter, I could not, in celebrating the Holy Eucharist, act in any way differently from the custom among us, without risk of giving pain or occasioning displeasure in the minds of others, at a time when, of all times, one should wish every thought to be of collectedness, devotion, stillness, peace. Although, then, like our dear friend, John

Keble, I believe the position condemned by the Judicial Committee, to be that which is in accordance with the Rubric and most in harmony with that highest act of our worship, I have felt obliged to abstain from a practice, which I should myself have preferred, in the cathedral where alone I can make myself responsible. I cannot, then, personally feel the judgment or opinion of the Judicial Committee as others do ; not so much because I cannot, without breach of charity, make myself amenable to it, if ever it shall become law, as because, in celebrating the solemn Sacrament and Sacrifice of the Eucharist, I have not been able to adopt the position which it condemns, except when ministering, accidentally, in churches or private chapels, where it was recognized by the congregation as the natural expression of Eucharistic worship. We, the older Tractarians, acted, you know, on the principle so wonderfully carried out by S. Cyprian, in times as difficult in their way as our own, first to win the minds of the people.

But, although this peculiarity of my own position has made it the more difficult for me to express an opinion, when asked, in that I cannot, as others, subject myself to the temporal consequences of passive resistance, I do feel the gravity of this judgment, not in itself, but in consequences or results which loom at no great distance. I do not (as I am sure that neither do you) ascribe any *conscious* partiality or want of justice to those members of the Judicial Committee who concurred in the recent judgment. But we are men ; not

fallible only, but with our several strong bias
which may unconsciously warp our judgment.
Such bias we thought that there was in previous
judgments, as well as in this. ·No one scarcely
doubted at the time that there was such a bias
in the Gorham judgment. It was commonly
supposed that the existence of the so-called Evangelical party in the Church of England depended
upon the issue of that judgment ; that they would,
if the Judicial Committee should confirm the judgment of the Ecclesiastical Court, be compelled
(unless they should reconsider and adopt the truth
which they had not yet received, or which .they
denied) to leave the Church of England. It was a
surprise, I remember, to some concerned on the
other side, to find that the judgment would, in an
opposite way, affect some of ourselves. It was, in
general, thought that the Gorham judgment was
meant as a measure of peace ; and, while judges
held (as Mr. Justice Parke said privately) that we
were the "righter" of the two, they thought that
the Evangelical Clergy were not absolutely excluded.
Certainly, one can hardly imagine how men of
judicial mind could, except under some strong bias,
think that when the Church required the Clergy, as
part of the Baptismal Service, to thank Almighty
God that "He had been pleased to regenerate this
infant," that it said this "in the judgment of charity"
—charity in this case, towards Almighty God, that
He gives to each infant with the Sacrament the grace
of the Sacrament which He had promised to give, the
infant being incapable of presenting any obstacle to

that grace. Equally, in the " Essays and Reviews"
case, it seemed impossible that any Court could take
the word "everlasting" in a non-natural sense of
not "lasting for ever," or assume that "the Word
of God" was, in grave matters too, not "God's
Word," unless there had been some strong bias not
to declare those doctrines to be the certain doctrines
of the Church of England.

In these cases the Judicial Committee had severally
carried to the extreme the principle that, in a
criminal cause, the balance must in every case of
doubt—*i.e.*, when a doubt can be felt or imagined—
be given in favour of the accused.   "A judgment,"
said the late acute Bishop Jeune to me, "will never
be given against any clergyman, unless he in terms
denies what the Articles affirm, or affirms what the
Articles deny." This he said in reference to the
indictment against Professor Jowett, which was
begun and quashed in its outset.

The Purchas judgment seems, if unchecked, likely
to inaugurate a new phase of these trials.   Hitherto
it had been ruled that the benefit of any possible
doubt should be given to the accused. You will
remember how often this was laid down in the judgment of Dr. Lushington, and consequently how
many of the complaints against the Essayists were
struck out in the Ecclesiastical Court. The Judicial
Committee completed what he began, and acquitted
them even as to those things, upon which Dr.
Lushington said that he was forced to condemn them.

In the Purchas judgment everything of this sort
disappeared. The suit, in that costs were decreed

against Mr. Purchas, was highly penal, compelling, if enforced, a Clergyman to pass, at least, through the Bankruptcy Court, if not ruining himself and his family. Yet even Sir J. T. Coleridge, with all the responsibility attaching to him as a member of the Privy Council, says, "I venture to say Mr. Purchas has not had justice done to him in two main points of the late appeal"—an appeal made not by him but against him, to obtain a conviction against him on those points upon which the Ecclesiastical Court had acquitted him. And those ruinous costs were given against him because he had been condemned in all, except some unimportant points (such as the wearing of a biretta); whereas, according to Sir J. T. Coleridge, on two main points he ought not to have been condemned. Why was not "justice" done to him? *You* do not think, or say, that there was any *conscious* bias in the minds of the judges. No one has, in any other case, questioned any judgment of Lord Hatherley's. Whence can have been, in this one case, this failure of justice, in a clear-minded lawyer, as to two main points of a cause brought before him? Whence this abandonment of the principle, so steadily adopted in previous judgments of the same Court, but from some *unconscious* bias—a natural bias in the minds of upright men, who may have dreaded that grave confusion might ensue if the practices impugned had been pronounced to be those sanctioned by the Court of England, and so were indisposed to see that they were so?

Sir J. T. Coleridge has pointed out the baselessness

of the decision on two of those points. To me, who have not studied matters of ritual, still more extraordinary appears to be the condemnation of the mixed chalice. There is no question that our Blessed Lord instituted the Holy Eucharist in wine, mingled with water;[1] it was wine mingled with water which He called "this fruit of the vine." The Judicial Committee pronounces that the Church of England prohibits the celebration of the Holy Eucharist as our Blessed Lord instituted it; and that, on the single ground that it calls "wine" what He, speaking of a mixed chalice, calls "the fruit of the vine." Water, of course, in that slight quantity which is infused into the mixed chalice, does not cause it to cease to be wine, any more than the infusion of alcohol in the wine prepared for our English market. Bishop Andrewes, who was born in 1555, had means of knowing what was the mind and practice of those days better than we, three centuries later. Yet he held the mixed chalice to be so intended, or at least approved, by the Church of England, that he inquired officially whether his Clergy so celebrated. The Judicial Committee had this testimony before them, but dismissed it in an offhand manner. So wedded were they to their own interpretation of the word "wine," that again, in a suit involving penalties, they would not give us even the benefit of a doubt, and a Clergyman was to be censured because he adopted a practice which, even after the Reformation, Bishop Andrewes would have blamed him for not adopting. I was at pains, many years

---

[1] *See* in Lightfoot, Horæ Hebraicæ, on 1 Matt. xxvi. 26.

ago, to point out that the Sacrament, in unmixed wine, was valid.[1] Certainly, no one versed in the subject could think that the Church of England, in adopting the ordinary name of the element, "wine," could have meant to prohibit that mode of celebration which our Lord used. Doubtless the Judicial Committee had either not known, or had forgotten this. But then, are those who condemn as illegal what our Blessed Lord did, competent to judge in these matters?

It is true that, in the Purchas case, no matter of faith has been impugned. Others have observed, how carefully every question of doctrine has been avoided. But when a Supreme Court pursues two such opposite courses in regard to causes brought before it, on former occasions using an extreme of strictness of construction, in order to avoid condemning those who appealed to it, and now an extreme laxity which brings about the condemnation of those whose accusers bring them before it, to obtain the reversal of a judgment in their favour, who could help misgivings about any question of doctrine which should come before it? Certainly, down to this last judgment, I scarcely thought it possible that, even though undefended, the case of Mr. Bennett could be given against him. I did indeed feel that I was treated like Uriah the Hittite, having been put by Mr. Bennett in the forefront of the battle, and there left, unable, by the forms of law, to defend myself, and undefended, even in the Archbishop's Court, by

[1] S. Cyprian's Epistles. Ep. 63, p. 189, note *d*. ("Library of the Fathers.")

himself or his advocate. I thought that the Church Association showed consciousness of the weakness of their cause when they refused to include me directly in the prosecution, while they attacked me indirectly by making two of the counts against Mr. Bennett his adoption of my words. *Now*, he must be more than man who could predict what the Judicial Committee will do. I should have misgivings if I, in the least, cared what its decision may be, except as regards the judges, that they may not condemn God's truth. If in an undefended cause it should pronounce as slovenly and unjudicial a judgment as it did in the suits against Mr. Mackonochie and Mr. Purchas, it might, by affirming any heresy, condemn us and itself. To what end? We have, happily, not all one neck for its guillotine to cut off. The Church Association would have, Tarquin-like, to cut off man by man. If it should eject us from our temporalities—me from Christ Church, you from St. Paul's, Carter from Clewer, and some hundreds of other laborious Clergy, from " spending themselves, and being spent " in the service of Christ, you and I should not have less influence with the youth of Oxford because we had suffered temporal loss for the truth of Christ; laborious Parish-priests have field enough, the harvest being plenteous, the labourers few. The Court would be tired of condemning sooner than we of being condemned. The Archbishop's Court having pronounced in our favour, that the doctrine which we have taught is (as we know) in harmony with the formularies of the Church of England, it would not matter to us

what a State-created Court, which can only take
away home and income, our. temporalities, may
decide. Nor will even this be an easy matter. The
judgment of the Supreme Court holds only, I understand, as long as the Court itself remains unchanged.
Its judgment would bind the Archbishop's Court
only as to the *ipsissima verba*, which it condemns.
Unless a term, like the Homöousion, is *the* term laid
down by the Church, we may vary our language
while teaching the self-same truths. A Fabian
policy will *cunctando restituet rem.* Men who are
prepared to part with everything except the Faith
will wear out even the Church Association. A few
more such victories will be its defeat and disgrace.

But, meanwhile, the Church Association has already
overreached itself, and, vaulting too high, has fallen
over on the other side. It has already included too
many in the condemnation. It has driven us into
a compact phalanx, which it will find difficult to
break.

II. I know not whether I am to interpret some of
my friend's words as counselling submission to this
judgment, if ever it should become, what as yet it
is not, law. It is not for me, who cannot expose
myself to its penalties, to counsel those to resist, who
might thereby forfeit the sphere of some twenty or
thirty years of labour and love. Yet I cannot but
see that the passive resistance which the Clergy
seem minded, far and wide, to show, may prevent
much greater evil and confusion, which would
ensue if the Judicial Committee were, in the
Bennett case also, to reverse the judgment of the

Ecclesiastical Court. I have been surprised to hear of grave persons counselling obedience to the Purchas judgment as matter of conscience, if it should become law, or even yielding obedience to it, while as yet it is not law. We have been in a state of continual protest against the Judicial Committee for these twenty-one years. Every Clergyman who has taught his people that Baptismal Regeneration is the doctrine of the Church of England; every Clergyman, who, in teaching the Church Catechism, teaches each child, one by one, to say, " in my Baptism, wherein I was made a member of Christ, a child of God, and an inheritor of the kingdom of heaven," emphatically contravenes that judgment. Every Clergyman who teaches that those who, to the end, shut out the grace of God, are lost for ever, or that God's word is indeed the Word of God, emphatically contradicts the "Essays and Reviews" judgment. The 11,000 Clergy who signed our Oxford Declaration, energetically contradicted it. Nay, the Church of England itself virtually contradicts both judgments. For, were the terms which it uses ambiguous as the State-Court would make them, it would have been wrong in the Church of England to continue to use them. It could not have dared to continue to require of us to pray over our departed, " deliver us not into the bitter pain of eternal death," had she not held that there is " an eternal death," into which they who, finally in this life, face to face, reject God, shall be cast. It could not have made us thank God with an illusive thanksgiving for having regenerated each infant, unless she believed that He gave what it depends on His merciful promise alone to give. The Privy Council has crippled discipline, and perhaps set some consciences at ease in denying the truth ; it has not in the least impaired the teaching of the Church for teachable minds, who take plain words in their plain sense. It is, then, a marvel to me to hear of grave persons all at once counselling obedience to this judge-made law, when we have for twenty-one years been, in another case, persistently contradicting it. Contradiction in word may be even more emphatic, and show more of "contempt of Court," than a silent disregard of it.

III. But as to the Court itself. My friend Sir J. T. Coleridge reminds us of the difficulty in which we are placed, that, if we would get rid of this Court, we must be subject to another ; and alludes to some of the difficulties in the Court to which we once looked, a Provincial Council of Bishops. Certainly I felt the difficulties which he suggests, when we proposed it twenty-one years ago. If the Provincial Synod should decide wrong, the consequences would be far graver. Yet I advocated it as being the legitimate Court of Appeal, trusting that, if it should be so constituted as was recommended, " in grave causes," in the "Reformatio legum Ecclesiasticarum," God the Holy Ghost, who made Bishops, would guide the Council convened in His Name. But there is a shorter course, which I have been glad to see advocated by one of a mind so calm as our old friend Archdeacon Churton, viz., that the Privy Council should be made simply a Civil Court. I should myself prefer that the Church of England should volunteer to place itself herein on the same footing as every other religious body in England. The State *will* interfere in every case where property is concerned ; and no harm would have ensued, had the State, *as* the State, retained to Mr. Wilson or Mr. R. Williams their respective incomes and parsonages. The mischief in all these decisions has been the quasi-ecclesiastical character of the Court, given to it by the presence of Archbishops or Bishops. Any increase of the ecclesiastical element, any reference to irresponsible theologians as assessors, any selection of Bishops as judges, would only make things worse. No one would have been disturbed by any judgment which Lord Campbell, or Lord Westbury, or Lord Cairns might have thought right to give, as Civil Judges. What shook minds through and through, when our eyes were opened by the Gorham judgment to the claims made by this Court, and what sent so many of our friends from us, and turned servants and sons of the Church into its deadliest antagonists, was, that a State-appointed Court claimed, in the name of the Church, the supervision and determination of its doctrine. A judgment in the Court of Queen's Bench might injure discipline ; it could not in any way commit the Church. It would be an interpretation of her formularies by Civil Judges pronouncing upon her teaching, but not in her name. In such case it would not matter whether the judge was of some dissenting body (as the lay members of the Judicial Committee may anyhow mostly be). Those without the Church are often better, because more disinterested, judges of the Church's doctrine than biassed members of the Church. No Dissenter, if elevated to the Bench, would have denied that the Church of England taught "the soul-destroying doctrine of Baptismal Regeneration," with which they reproach her; but, anyhow, such could not speak in the name of the Church. It would be but like the appeal to the heathen Emperor Aurelian as to the see-house of Antioch. Moreover, since such an appeal would only be to the State, to do justice to one who thought himself wronged in temporals, it could not be turned to the oppression of the accused. The prosecutor would, I suppose, have no appeal. Such a Court would have retained the temporalities of Mr. Gorham, Mr. Wilson, and Mr. R. Williams; it could not have passed judgment against Mr. Mackonochie or Mr. Purchas for points upon which they had been acquitted by the Archbishop's Court, nor could the harass of renewed prosecution hang thus long over Mr. Bennett after he had been in like way acquitted. In asking for the abolition of all Ecclesiastical appeals to the Judicial Committee of the Privy Council, we should have the advantage of popular opinion, in that we should be asking nothing for ecclesiastics, no special privilege to the Church, but placing ourselves on a level with every other religious body.

IV. In regard to disestablishment, I have never yet used a word so strong as that of " *coöperation* with the political forces which, year by year, more and more steadily are working towards disestablishment." But

F

simply, because I think it safer to leave a question
so grave in the hands of God's Providence, who, by
His overruling Spirit, brings His beautiful order out
of the chaos of the tumultuous wills of men.   Disestablishment would probably leave our towns much
as they are ; our universities are virtually half-dis-
established already, through the active cöoperation of
the Government.   But in view of the sufferings and
privations, temporal and spiritual, of our villages,
such as Sir J. T. Coleridge hints at, I shrink from
actively partaking in a measure which would entail
such consequences.   I shrink, too, from cöoperating
in what would probably involve large desecration of
what has been once given to God.   But it must in
itself much encourage those who are bent on dis-
establishing the Church, that a large, and, I may
say, thoughtful section of the Church will take no
part in opposing their efforts, nay, will rather look
upon them as deliverers from the truth-oppressing
thraldom of the State.   Chains are not the less galling
because they are of gold, nor poison the less deadly,
because the pill is coated in silver. I need not recall
to you the occasion, upon which, a year and a half
ago, I too expressed nearly the same feeling as you
have now as to disestablishment. If things go on in
the same wild way, in which men are now impelling
them, those of us whom God shall continue on here
may have to take the side which you anticipate. Things
look that way, both within and without the Church.
A Convocation—meddling with grave questions, and
setting grave precedents, changing our public service,
as far, at least, as the Scriptures which we are to

read, and the burial of our dead, compelling us, it seems, to omit, or admit, of its good pleasure ; committing the revision of our Scriptures to a body, consisting in part of those whose excuse, in the sight of God, is an invincible prejudice against doctrines which those Scriptures teach,—and yet not representing nor consulting the Clergy, whom it proposes to compel by penal enactment to accept its decisions, does not inspire the wish that such a body should continue State-imposed. A State-appointed Commission, which threatened us (but that God withheld it,) with the privation of that wondrous guide of faith and of thought, the Athanasian Creed, inspires us with no wish for the continuance of an establishment in which such State-meddling is possible.

I need not dwell upon other evils. There are chronic evils, such as the high-handed appointment of our Bishops (lately, against the protest of most Clergy of a Diocese ; formerly, against a formal protest of Bishops), the sale of advowsons or next presentations, the hindrance of discipline, which nothing probably but disestablishment will cure. Disestablishment must, after the precedent of the Irish Church, come sooner or later. It may be the question, not of establishment, with its balance of good and evil, as our friend sees it, but of disestablishment, before the Church is corrupted, or after. Judgment upon judgment presses this still more upon us. Our forbearance is stretched more and more, till the tension may be too great. We may be driven (and God only knows how soon) to decide whether it be right and faithful to our God

" propter vitam vivendi perdere causas," for the sake
of an establishment which has such a fleeting life, to
see *that* wrested from us which alone gives to establishments their value. And this alone I understand
you to mean.

May God guide you in the coming crisis, which
perhaps may come ere I, too, part hence, though
also perhaps not.

Your most affectionate friend,
E. B. PUSEY.

Monday in Holy Week, 1871.

P.S.—And now, when I have scarce closed my
letter, the first signs of the ensuing contest are
showing themselves. We Englishmen have a
strange power of blinding ourselves to what we do
not like to see, and a strange fondness for throwing
dust into others' eyes. Scarce had the words been
uttered, "the University Tests Bill and the Burial Bill
passed, I hope we shall hear no more of Dissenters'
grievances," than the new claims were raised. To
us, who observed how the overtures to the believing
Dissenters were met by them, it became clear that
their object in supporting the University Tests Bill
was not any gain to themselves, but the assertion of
their political equality with the Church of England.
They disdained solid advantages,—the founding of
Colleges of their own out of the revenues of the existing Colleges, in proportion to their numbers and their
needs, with the same position as our own,—because
they used the University Tests Bill as a stepping-

stone, holding itself and its professed objects as cheap as men do the ground which supports them. They allowed their names to be used, as though they desired to be admitted to Fellowships which they knew that (except here and there) not they, but the hard-headed and well-trained deniers of the Faith or of all religion would gain, because the bill would so far establish what alone they cared for,—the principle of their political equality with the Church of England. To us then it was clear that the disestablishment of the Universities (as far as the bill went) was a means, not an end; an instalment, yet a fraction only, of those further unconcealed claims. The "important Nonconformist meeting," under the presidency of Mr. Miall, was a remarkable union of those who dissented from each other in everything except their antagonism to Establishments. English Presbyterians were willing to sacrifice the ascendancy of their body in Scotland, if only they could, by the same blow, destroy the political ascendancy of the Church of England. Those who denied and those who believed in Christ crucified, united during the week of His Passion, if so they might disestablish the Church, which eminently in all her worship confesses and impresses It upon her people. Melancholy, yet only too natural a combination for an end of human ambition, but not the less strong for ends of this world, because religiously unnatural! Conservatives, County-Members, Broad-Church, Erastians, will have enough to do to maintain a "National Church" against the stress of the assault of a body, combining the motley forces of the varied religionists and antireligionists, Deists, Atheists, Materialists. No need to impel a railway-engine from behind. But meanwhile our neutral position will command respect. We have a definite principle, zeal for the faith, indifference to all besides, and so, readiness to sacrifice all besides for the faith. Those whose zeal is for the Establishment, and who think that all besides will come right if *that* is maintained, know now on what terms our support is to be had. The battle must, I suppose, last some years. The Disestablishmentarians have occupied too wide a front, to carry all points at once, unless we, like Metz, surrender. Meanwhile, the prolongation of the conflict is the gain, as of the Church generally, so especially ours, who most faithfully represent it. My anxiety would begin when the disestablishment should be completed, lest the Evangelicals and ourselves should not understand one another. If the Evangelicals should, at the time of the disestablishment, still (though not secretly sympathizing) be under the dominion of the fanatic Church Association, the Church of England must break to pieces; the Evangelicals uniting themselves with the anti-Sacramentarians; the Broad-Church, as a body, with the anti-Trinitarians; and the more moderate of either uniting with ourselves. We are gaining, year by year, from both; and when the mists which have gathered through the stiffness or indiscretion and lordly claims of some of our friends, and still more through the frost-breath of journals which make themselves our organs, nipping all charity, and bitter towards all except themselves, shall have cleared away, minds will be more open to receive (as they are daily more and more receiving) the full, unshrouded, unimpaired light of the glorious Gospel. We have a glorious cause, the cause of God; and while we are diligent and watchful to guard the purity of the Faith unimpaired, may well, amid the visible growth and deepening of His work, " stand still and see the salvation of God."

Monday in Easter Week, 1871.

J. OGDEN AND CO., PRINTERS, 172, ST. JOHN STREET, E.C.